Cloak

To Jane and Robert,
in friendship.

love,

Susan xxx

London, 10 april 2022

Cloak

Poems by

Susan Castillo Street

Cover design by Shay Culligan

Cover photograph by

ISBN: 978-1-950462-84-1

Kelsay Books Inc.

kelsaybooks.com

502 S 1040 E, A119
American Fork, Utah 84003

For David

Acknowledgments

Some of the poems in this volume have appeared in the following journals and anthologies:

New Context: "Joined"

Ink Sweat & Tears: "Pact"

Firth: "Stanley"

Algebra of Owls: "Coin"

Ink Sweat & Tears: "Under the Volcano"

The New European: "Balkans" "Under the Volcano"

The Lake: "Trove" "Palimpsest"

Amaryllis: "Old Rocker"

Fairy Rings and Changelings: ed. Kate Garrett (Three Drops Press): "Fairies"

The Blue Nib: "Reading," "Apocalypse," "Test Match" "The Museum of Sophistication" "Palma"

I Am Not a Silent Poet: "I Would Like to Think"

"Bird of God", about the Pre-Raphaelite painter Joanna Boyce, was published in the *Pre-Raphaelite Review* and won first prize in the Pre-Raphaelite Society Poetry Competition

Contents

III.

I.

Cloak

You're made of different strands:
      green threads of Sussex fields
      swirling Mississippi currents
      blue drifts of foreign skies.

Sometimes you sit light on my shoulders:
      shimmer of Balkan sun
       woven thick with distant music
      voices purling down the street

Other times you weigh me down:
      black knots unravelling
      grey absence comes in waves
      dark swells of sea and whitecap sighs.

I've grown used to you, old cloak,
      yet find it reassuring that
      one day I'll smile and cast you off
      watch you floating into sky.

Shield

In the twilight, I lie against
my father's chest, breathe smells
of peppermints and sweat.

The chair creaks as we rock back and forth.
Over his shoulder, I see wicker
patterned with black squares.

He sings of sentimental journeys,
bids blackbirds bye-bye. I lean my head
against his ribs, feel their thrum,

hear the drumbeat of his heart,
know I am sheltered, safe,
swathed in my father's arms.

Train

Hot summer night, back garden,
firefly-spangled, sloping down to the bayou.
From a window in the town jail,
a harmonica wails of love,

oh love oh careless love.

The chirr of crickets.
In the distance, we can hear a distant train
the Dixie Special, ooooOOOOOOOOOoooo
Doppler blues fading into dark.

Trove

Clearing my mother's house,
I empty out her handbag, find

     a tasseled cigarette,
     a lipstick labeled Fire and Ice,
     a steno pad with cryptic scrawls
     a photograph of me aged five

     a tissue blotted with a kiss.

Blended Family

In the back garden, posed before
an apple tree. From left to right:
me, baby with Chinese Emperor frown,
held in my father's arms.

My father. Big tall man, broad shoulders,
Quizzical air. At his side, my mama,
hair tumbling round her shoulders,
plump, pretty. Between them both, my stepbrother,

all buck teeth and towhead spikes.
Standing by him, my stepsister, halter top
and ruffled skirt, arms akimbo.
Her look says *Don't mess with me.*

Making people stand together smiling
for a moment just to make a pretty picture,
is artistic licence, I suppose. Bringing us close,
smoothing awkward angles, erasing the dark shadows.

for one golden moment
we are woven close together
standing in the sunlight,
blended, whole.

Joined

Parham Plummer Bridges, 1829-1886
Penelope Thompson Bridges, 1832-1876

They married young. In church, he saw her
smiling over her left shoulder. That was it.
Here, they're standing side by side. His eyes blaze blue.
His beard unfurls, proclaims possession.

Her face is curved and pointed like a heart.
Her hair is black, pulled back.
Her eyes look fearless out at us.
Her sister said he wore her out:

eleven children, twenty years.
Two died small. Parham Plummer went to war,
in '62 was taken prisoner. Penelope farmed the land,
and fed them all. When peace arrived,

they travelled west, claimed land in wild Sabine.
Then Penny died. Though he married once again
and sired two children, Parham lies there close:
he and Penny, buried side by side.

Claim

To Jacob Monroe Pierce, 1833-1898
and Mary Matilda MacMahon Pierce, 1842-1908

Seated side by side, they look out at us.
She in flowing, homespun dress,
hair pinned back in a tight knot.
He, formal in a suit with waistcoat,
hand draped over Bible.

Her fingers clasp his shoulder.
Her eyes are Texas flint.
Her look would drill cold metal, says
     This is my man.

Jacob made it through the War,
came home in in 1865, then
fell from a horse and died.
Mary Matilda did not break.

Grim, dour, she prayed for his soul
through thick dark Southern nights.
Years later, she joined him there
staked her claim to Texas soil.

Silt

William Friend McMahon, 1748-1794

McMahon men grow tall.
I was six foot six. That made me
an easy target, head above the rest.

My men dug a grave inside the fort,
lay me there. I could not rest.
There in the dark, the Indians whisper.

Little Turtle and his men
mocking me. *You are not our Friend,*
White man, Indian Killer This land is ours.

I try in vain to speak.
> *God made this land for us*
> *Not for you heathens*
My mouth is full of silt.

Later, my family took me home
buried me close by the church.
They knew these bones were me,

tall lanky skeleton, a bullet hole
between black sockets where eyes used to be.

Solos, 1990

In our bell jars
mouths move
but we can't hear

we reach out, touch only distance
look at each other
see empty air

the worst alone
is when we're with someone
who isn't really there.

My Hair

Peach candyfloss fuzz.
Long pigtails (used to flagellate school bullies in propeller
motion).
Teenage ponytail. Jackie Kennedy helmet, spray-shellacked,
bouffant.

Straight hippy hair. I used to iron it.
Pixie do. With babies there's no time for more.
Jennifer Aniston layers, dyed red. What was I thinking.

Highlights, relatively sedate, expensive.
Silver, settling into white.
Celebrating white.

Equation

Sooner or later, all loves
      end in death,
      slope down to disappointment,
      fade into distance.

Our capacity to love,
      let down barriers, trust,
      look into another's eyes,
      find safe haven there

is directly proportional
to our capacity for pain
when love is ripped away.
As we skate on melting ice

the singing in our veins
persuades us loving's worth the risk
of the abyss, of all the pain
that comes with loss.

Brazilians have a saying for this paradox:
      O amor é eterno enquanto dura
      Love is eternal
      as long as it lasts.

Voices

Ghosts have their uses.
They can be used as blankets
to keep us from the cold.

We can hide beneath them,
wrap ourselves in phantom sheets
as camouflage to ward off predators,

cloak ourselves in spectral duvets
made of memories no one can take away.
Still, we mustn't let the voices of our ghosts

smother what is happening in the now,
seal our ears to second chances
to hear the magic of new music.

Gomera

Somehow it seems a fitting site
to celebrate this zero year.
Looking out at the horizon,

there's a finality about this place,
a lightness, a jumping-off.
The Genovese set out from here,

sails pregnant with ambition,
greed and faith. I ask myself
what lies beyond the thin blue threshold,

whether one day I'll sail off
to an Indies full of gold and light
or coast the whirlpool down

to face large shapes of monsters
lurking in the silent dark.
I laugh and surf the swirl.

Rippling Spring

A south wind combs the meadow grass.
Waves of light and shadow flow toward me,
break against the wooden fence.

I look out through my window,
cup hands around a mug of tea,
savour the insideness.

Outside, chill lingers. Still I feel
a burgeoning, a hint of a relentless thing
pushing, pushing, through the soil and stones.

Something wild and glorious
lurks untamed in rippling spring,
warm breath, a humming in my bones.

II.

Stanley

I float into the kitchen, lured by the scent of bacon.
I wonder if Doris knows I'm here, does this
to torment me with smells of pleasures
I no longer taste. Her mouth is pursed.
Her perm's as prim as ever.

The circumstances of my death
were compromising, I admit. I died savouring the delights
of Lily from Accounting.
Doris was not best pleased.
She smiles, slashes fragrant rashers.

Palimpsest

The old Greek gods are written
in our sinews, sing in our blood.
Our lips draw tight in Cupid bows.
Our eyes hold rainbow Irises.

Atop our spine, the Atlas vertebra
holds up our weighty skull, globe balanced
on a butterfly of bone. Below, the mount of Venus
rises resplendent, conceals Hymen's shielded door.

Achilles heeled, we think we're armed against it all,
fire our arrows, garland ourselves in light,
climb peaks, think that the gods
will never let us fall.

The Museum of Sophistication

Cole Porter tinkles in a corner.
Ava Gardner's feather boa prickles, tickles.
A dummy of Coco Chanel is corseted in tweed

and pearls. Grace Kelly's glamour's sheathed in ice.
She drives men wild. They think
they'll be the one to make her thaw.

Marlene Dietrich's hat and cane
sheathed in seductive cruelty,
nicht wahr?

Marilyn Monroe's lipstick
puckers pink.
ooh-poo-pa-doo.

I wanna be loved by you
Alone.

Bibliogenesis

Books breed in corners,
teeming, mating, making other books.
They accumulate in twisting orgiastic ziggurats.

When the lights go off
the things they get up to!
Shocking, really.

They leap off the shelves,
cavort in dark nooks,
flutter their pages at one another

The most unsuitable things occur:
       Dorothy Parker hangs out with Fenimore Cooper,
       just her bit of rough. Emily Dickinson gets it on
       with Walt Whitman, though one would have thought
       they were not that way inclined.
       Still, who knows. Truman Capote
       bats his lashes at Mark Twain.
       Fat thrillers hiss conspiracies, explosions.

We think we're in control.
But when we conclude
a major purge is much to be desired

to get a grip on this appalling
misbehaviour, books snigger in the dark.
I take bags and bags

of 70s feminist theory, Heidegger,
Aristotle, deconstruction, lit crit,
silly novels, to the charity shop, but

suddenly, like the tides,
the books just flow back in,
start frolicking again.

Supping at Emmaus

The two disciples walk toward Emmaus
with heavy tread. They left their Master
torn and broken, sealed in stone by Roman hands.

As night falls, they ask a stranger they encounter
on the way to come and dine with them.
In the village inn, the lights are dim.

The landlord and his wife lay out solid fare,
prepare to leave them. Suddenly
the stranger blazes bright, then ripples back

into the blackest dark. Luke and Cleophas blink,
transfixed, ask themselves how it can be
that boundaries between dimensions are so porous,

how it is possible for divine beauty
to transcend the night, for light to shimmer
into dusty worlds of bread and sweat and aching feet.

Apocalypse

The day the world ends
I get up early, go downstairs,
 swear at cats, stroke cats.
I put on a jacket, walk down to the gate,
pick up the papers. I read about
the disasters politicians have inflicted
on us, tut over celebrity misbehavior,
check email, eat breakfast, drink many cups
of coffee. I make a list for the supermarket,
walk out to the car, put the key in the ignition,
look up at the sky, note that it's turned
a weird dark sepia shade. And then I

Apple

I scatter flour on the granite,
roll out dough, drape it over tin,
prick it with a fork, flute the edges.

In a bowl are six sweet spheres.

Three are Braeburn, three are Cox.
The Braeburn globes glisten.
The Cox are golden, tart.
I'm making pie for two small girls.

My mind drifts off to ancient Greece.
I ask myself why Paris found it hard
to judge which goddess is deserving
of his prize:

> Motherly Hera, who tends his hearth.
> Boring. Then there's Athena,
> more clever than himself.
> Predictably, he chooses sexy Aphrodite.

I peel the apples, core and slice them,
sprinkle cinnamon and sugar, fan crescents
out in spirals, dot with butter, open oven door,
put pie to bake. The kitchen fills

with spicy scent. I sit down with a cup of tea,
think that now it's time
to let us women judge
who wins the golden apple.

Fairies

Don't tell them about fairies,
my scientist daughter says.
We're already overdoing it
with Santa and the Easter Bunny.

I get it, I really do. I understand
that we don't want to peddle lies.
But that's the thing:
I actually believe it's true

the world is full of magic:
unseen spirits dancing in the flowers,
voices whispering in the wind.

How sad and gray the world
would be if just the 'real'
is all we see.

Bird of God

Joanna knew that yes meant sacrifice.
Domestic ties come first, even before art.
And what an artist she was, my Joanna.
Even Ruskin praised her work.

I courted her. We roamed the fields,
painted side by side. Perhaps she thought
if she accepted me, she could have motherhood
and art, not be forced to choose.

For a while, she had them both. I remember her
laughing, paint-stained, amid the smell of turps.
until the day she died in childbirth.
I put red roses on her pillow,

saw colour leach from her dear face,
took up a pencil, drew its planes,
her strong profile, her brows,
her wings of wild black hair. Wanting to do her justice,

I asked Rossetti to make another sketch.
His words hit me like stones:

> *A great artist sacrificed to bring*
> *another child into the world,*
> *as if there were not more women* .
> *just fit for that task.*

Old Rocker

He sits in front of a blue piano,
ancient rhino in the cross hairs,
blinking in the spotlights.

He leans forward, touches keys,
eases into surfin' safaris,
dreams of golden California girls.

Melancholy swirls around him
rising like blue smoke.
God he's ancient I think. Time to go to bed.

I turn off the telly, head upstairs,
glance in the mirror,
grimace when I see

a strange old woman
peering back at me.

Under the Volcano

23 June 2016

In the distance, Mt. Etna rises,
summit veiled in smoke
and clouds. Below, fields ripple out,
fold into deep blue valley.

I sit at a café on the square.
Passeggiata crowds surge and swirl.
Two men strum plaintive mandolins.
At a nearby table, a tourist reads his news.

Bold headlines blare and blast,
boast of regained sovereignty.
It all seems so remote here
on this island in the sun.

I look to the horizon,
feel beneath my feet
the trembling ground,
the coming rain of liquid fire.

I Would Like to Think

I would like to think
My fellow citizens believe in fairness,
sporting chances, helping underdogs.

I would like to think
our arms are open to those fleeing war
in search of sanctuary.

I would like to think
this country is a place where children
have enough to eat and grow.

I would like to think
we stand for values such as
tolerance, civility, compassion.

I would like to think
we have the sense to vote for leaders
who are not corrupt buffoons.

I would like to think
we are a nation of sane people
who do the right thing in the end.

III.

At First Sight

Logic would fall
out of its chair laughing
at this bolt from the blue nonsense.

There are scientific explanations
for this absurd syndrome,
this head over heels malarkey:

> longing
> sheer boredom
> projection

What a ridiculous concept
until it happens.

Rainbows

She wants blue skies
He wants red roses

She wants yellow suns
He wants green grass

She wants globes of orange fruit
He wants clouds fringed in violet

She wants indigo water ripples
He wants silver leaves

In a sun-drenched London garden
they collide.

The world explodes in rainbows

Coin

I saw a coin in the water
and thought it might be a goldfish
or a lost spangle of sun
or a wish made by lovers
or a gambler rolling the dice.

The Perfect Shape

A circle, all holding hands,
unity in equal, rational distance.
The sensible choice.

Spiral, spinning spinning.
Intense, passionate,
who knows where it will end.

I know which one I'd go for.

Un regalo de la vida

For D, Dubrovnik, August 2018.

Our eyes meet over the table.
Organ music wafts our way
from the concert in the square.

A Spanish phrase pops into mind:
Un regalo de la vida
I look away and blink. The world shimmers.

Here in this golden city by the sea
our fingers touch.

Cinquaine

Rain falls
softly. Wind howls.
Limbs entwined, we dive deep
into a world of eyes and touch.
One heart.

Balkans

Inside, the air is cold.
On the walls, a gallery of pain
in glossy black and white:

> people with dead eyes
> children staring out of wagons
> a woman in a bombed-out house
> bodies stacked like cords of firewood.

One photo grabs me by the throat:
a plump Roma child lies limp,
naked infant Christ. The label says

> *In the van, the child overheated*
> *could not be saved.*
> In the background,
> a mother's silent scream.

We go out to the sun
are swept into the tourist crowds
shiver, wonder if we'll ever learn.

Hearts

Hand in hand we walk
amid the ruins. Sun pours
off golden stones. Cicadas chirr.

The air is thick with ghosts.
Voices haggling in the market,
scolding children, laughing.

We look down at our feet.
On the ground, mosaics spiral,
trace vines, leaves shaped like interlacing hearts.

Catspeak

I perch on the arm of the sofa,
plump white sphinx. I glare at her,
telegraph *where the hell have you been.*

She doesn't speak cat, poor girl.
Since my rival came on the scene,
she walks around with goofy grin.

Still, he's not too bad as humans go.
We boys must stick together.
So I let him stroke me just a little.

After all, she serves our food on time.
But she mustn't get ideas above her station.

Crocked

You say, *We're crocked*
in similar ways. At first,
I take huge umbrage.
This is not the sort of gallantry
to which I am accustomed.
How very dare you.

On reflection, though, you have a point:
  Our knees are buckling or bionic
  Our eyes are dimming
  We wear our scars, we do.

But if between us we come up with
  one good eye out of four
  two walking legs
  two statin-laced but ardent hearts,

it seems to me we might just limp on
happily ever after
for a while.

Hands

Big hands
Warm hands
Gentle hands
Skillful hands

When we're hand in hand
you complete me.

Pact

The lawn's carpeted with yellow leaves.
Gardeners on a mission, we rake them
into doubloon mounds. The air is sharp and clear.
Our eyes meet. No need for words.
I hold this closeness fast,
know that winter's on its way.
I'd sell my soul to make this moment last

Old Lovers

After breakfast, I grumble.
Tupperware vanishes from my house
purloined by my children.

You come riding to the rescue.
I have lots of Tupperware
if you'd like to take a few.

In the middle of the kitchen.
our edges fit
as we seal tight into each other.

Test Match

We watch the cricket.
Clueless American, British man.

I blink at the screen, hesitate, ask
sorry, but, er, what is a wicket?

He smiles back,
explains *leg in front, googly.*

I remind myself that after all,
he has passed the Elvis Test.

A man who's Sound on Elvis
and a woman deciphering cricket

may indicate a willingness
to speak and maybe even love

each other's language.

Palma

The sun pours down like honey,
flows off golden walls while
people eddy. From a window,
guitar chords ripple, cascade.

In the middle of the square, an olive tree
stands solid, flamenco dancer
of a certain age. Her bark spirals, swirls.
Her *traje de volantes* flutters in the wind.

No fragile sapling, but solid,
weathered, infinitely lovely. Wind shimmers
in silver leaf hair. Olives rain down,
castanets clattering on stones.

Mantegna's Christ

Milan, Saturday before Easter
Tourists swirl in sparrow circles.
Headlines scream dark threats.
 In the coolness of the gallery, guides chatter.
We round a corner, stop in our tracks.

On a stone slab, Christ lies dead, legs foreshortened.
Blood oozes from the holes
the nails have left. His feet are callused, dusty.
His head is tilted to one side.
On the left, a cluster of three faces.

>   His mother Mary's lined with loss.
>   In profile, John the Beloved.
>   Emerging from the blackness
>   Mary Magdalene's silent scream.

He is very cold and dead, this Christ.
I ask myself if in these times of chaos,
we're condemned to forever grieve for what's been lost,
or if there's still hope for redemption
to blaze forth tomorrow morning.

Reading

I touch your skin
read you with my fingertips

sense your close-grained texture
feel the warmth that seeps

between the cells.
The current shoots up my arms

makes me want
to live and live and live.

Haiku

Dancing on the wind
white angel petal flutters
gossamer delight.

Monsaraz

The Sorceresses' Tower looms
in a corner of this walled city
looking outward toward Castille.
It juts against the sky.

I wonder what spells the witches cast.
Amid the stones, I glimpse a girl
with long black hair. She fades away
as tourists chatter, then emerges

once again, laughs and whispers in my ear,
tells me that some fools view living stones
and earth and ghosts and fairy rings
as separate things.

Estatuas yacientes

We lie there holding hands.
Two reclining statues,
Medieval knight. his lady.

In my dreams I spend eternity
warm marble
resting at your side.

Calling Time

We look out over the valley.
This pub has been here for four hundred years.
Wars wash back and forth. Ghosts hover.
Kings, Spitfires, armies in the Wealden mist.

Indoors, we sit around the table,
family out for Sunday roast.
A white-haired man and woman,
A youngish couple, two little girls.

Horse brasses glint around the fire,
On the wall above our heads
An ancient clock ticks. On its dial, two words:
Tempus fugit.

Approaching Winter

We hurtle through the countryside,
whiz through suburban stations.
Commuters line the plaforms,
black clothespins all in rows.

Through rain-specked windows
autumn whooshes by:
blasts of russet, bursts of gold,
swathes of flickering scarlet.

Beside me, a man reads his paper.
Another fiddles with his phone. A baby yowls.
I find it weirdly comforting

to think that all of us are heading
relentlessly down the tracks
toward a shared darkness.

About the Author

Susan Castillo Street is Harriet Beecher Stowe Professor Emeritus, King's College, University of London. She has published three collections of poems, *The Candlewoman's Trade* (Diehard Press, 2003), *Abiding Chemistry,* (Aldrich Press, 2015) and *The Gun-Runner's Daughter* (Kelsay Books, 2017, and a pamphlet *Constellations* (Three Drops Press, 2015). Her poems have been published widely in the US, the UK, Mexico, South Africa and Luxembourg, in *Southern Quarterly, The Missing Slate, The Lake, Ink Sweat & Tears, Firth, I Am Not a Silent Poet, The New European, Messages in a Bottle, The Yellow Chair Review, Three Drops in a Cauldron, York Mix* and *The Blue Nib,* among others. She was born in the American South, but lives between London and East Sussex.

I would like to express my gratitude to Sarah Miles, Sian Thomas, Lawrence Wilson, Jill Munro and Louisa Campbell; to Deborah Alma and to the Deadline Poets Society; to Wendy Pratt for her excellent prompts, and to my fellow pirates on the Coast of Bohemia.

Printed in Poland
by Amazon Fulfillment
Poland Sp. z o.o., Wrocław